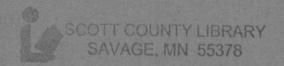

GETTING TO KNOW THE WORLD'S GREATEST ARTISTS

GIOTTO

WRITTEN AND ILLUSTRATED BY MIKE VENEZIA

CHILDREN'S PRESS®
A DIVISION OF GROLIER PUBLISHING
NEW YORK   LONDON   HONG KONG   SYDNEY
DANBURY, CONNECTICUT

For Vincent Xavier Venezia

Cover: *Lamentation of Christ,* by Giotto di Bondone. Scrovegni Chapel, Padua, Italy.
© Art Resource, NY/Scala.

Colorist for illustrations: Liz Venezia

Library of Congress Cataloging-in-Publication Data

Venezia, Mike.
    Giotto / written and illustrated by Mike Venezia.
        p.   cm. — (Getting to know the world's greatest artists)
    Summary: Discusses the life and work of Giotto, considered the most
important Italian artist of the fourteenth century.
    ISBN 0-516-21592-2 (lib. bdg.)   0-516-27040-0 (pbk.)
    1. Giotto, 1266?-1337 Juvenile literature. 2. Painters—Italy Biography
Juvenile literature. [1. Giotto, 1266?-1337. 2. Artists.] I. Title. II. Series:
Venezia, Mike. Getting to know the world's greatest artists.
ND623.G6V46 2000
759.5—dc21
[B]   99-41808
                                                                          CIP

Visit Children's Press on the Internet at:
http://publishing.grolier.com

Copyright 2000 by Mike Venezia.
Printed in the United States of America.
1 2 3 4 5 6 7 8 9 10 R 09 08 07 06 05 04 03 02 01 00

Giotto di Bondone was born around 1266 in a beautiful hilly farm area near Florence, Italy. Because Giotto lived so long ago, not all that much is known about his life. One thing most people are sure of, though, is that he was one of the greatest artists ever.

The reason there isn't a lot of information about Giotto is that hardly anyone knew how to read or write during his time.

Hundreds of years before Giotto was born, most of Europe was ruled by the Roman Empire. At that time, people were better educated. They loved art, beautiful buildings, and decorations. Then something terrible happened.

Armies of angry barbarians from
faraway lands wanted to take over wealthy
Roman cities throughout Europe. Finally,
in the year A.D. 476, after years of war,
they ended up beating the Roman armies.

Barbarians didn't care at all about reading or art. In fact, they destroyed statues, buildings, wall paintings and anything else they didn't understand!

From the end of the Roman Empire until Giotto's time, art slowly came back into style. But now it wasn't for the pleasure of decorating homes or city buildings. Art was used as a way of teaching religious stories to people who couldn't read.

Multiplication of the Loaves and Fishes, by unknown artist, c. 493-526. Byzantine mosaic. S. Apollinare Nuovo, Ravenna, Italy. © Art Resource, NY/Scala.

Crucifixion, by unknown artist. Byzantine mosaic. Monastery Church, Hosios Loukas, Greece. Photograph by Erich Lessing. © Art Resource, NY.

The rulers of the Catholic Church pretty much ran things in Europe now. They worked hard to convince barbarian tribes and others to behave themselves by following the teachings of Jesus Christ.

Artists began creating work for empty walls and domes of newly built churches all over Europe. They usually made paintings or mosaics. A mosaic is a picture made up of thousands of pieces of cut glass or stone.

Making the scenes look realistic wasn't important to artists or leaders of the church.

They felt it was more important to show
a symbolic story about Jesus, the saints,
and other religious people in a serious,
respectable way. Church leaders had strict
rules about how pictures were supposed
to look.

Figures in these works of art looked flat, almost like they were cut out and stuck onto the background. Artists never showed movement or gave their paintings a feeling of space or perspective.

The people in these works of art, with their mysterious, powerful eyes, are very beautiful, but they don't seem real at all. Paintings that felt more natural and alive weren't created until Giotto came along.

Madonna and Child, by Berlinghiero. Tempera on wood, gold ground. 76.2 x 49.5 cm. Gift of Irma N. Straus, 1960 (60.173). Photograph by Schecter Lee. © Metropolitan Museum of Art.

Giotto started a whole new style of painting. He painted religious stories too, but he began to put depth into his scenes so that things wouldn't look so flat.
He paid attention to the backgrounds, making buildings, forests, and mountains an important part of the picture.

Flight into Egypt, by Giotto di Bondone. c. 1305-06. Scrovegni Chapel, Padua, Italy. © Art Resource, NY/Scala.

The Meeting of Joachim and Anna at the Golden Gate, by Giotto di Bondone. c. 1305-06.
Scrovegni Chapel, Padua, Italy. © Archivi Alinari. © Art Resource, NY.

Most of all, Giotto di Bondone put human feeling into his figures. His people seem alive compared to paintings done by earlier artists. Giotto was probably the first European artist to show expressions of joy, anger, surprise, and sadness. His paintings also show he had a special understanding of nature.

Giotto probably learned all about nature when he was a small boy. A famous story tells how Giotto kept himself busy while watching his father's sheep. Giotto studied and drew pictures of flowers, mountains, pine trees, and animals he saw in the countryside near his home.

He used a sharp stone to scratch out scenes on large, flat rocks. One day, Cimabue, the greatest Italian artist of the day, was traveling through the area and saw Giotto drawing. Cimabue couldn't believe his eyes. He had never seen a young boy creating such wonderful art.

Cimabue immediately offered to take Giotto to his famous workshop in the city of Florence.

No one knows if this story is true, but most experts agree that at an early age, Giotto did learn all about art in Cimabue's workshop. It must have been an exciting time for Giotto. Florence, Italy, was one of the greatest art cities in the world. It was filled with all kinds of busy artists.

Boys who learned from master artists were called apprentices. They started by learning about everything having to do with art. It wasn't an easy life. Apprentices also had to keep the workshop clean and do laundry and lots of other chores. Sometimes it took years before an apprentice was ready to be a real artist.

Saint Gregory the Great, School of Giotto di Bondone. Church of Saint Francis, upper level, Assisi, Italy. © Art Resource, NY/Scala.

It seems that even as an apprentice, Giotto was good enough to assist Cimabue and help him paint important works in different cities in Italy.

People were amazed by the realism in Giotto's work. Early on, Giotto became known around Italy as a remarkable artist. It wasn't long before Giotto became a master artist with a workshop and assistants of his own.

Isaac Rejecting Esau, School of Giotto di Bondone. Church of Saint Francis, Assisi, Italy. © Art Resource, NY/Scala.

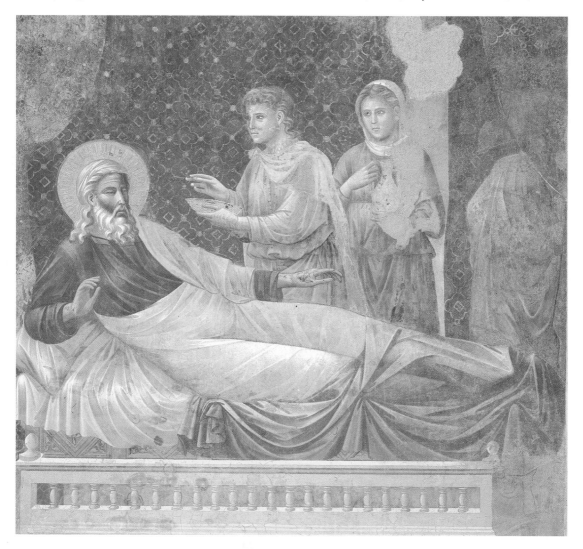

Some of Giotto's first known important paintings are in the Church of St. Francis in Assisi, Italy. They are stories about the kind and caring saint who had lived in Assisi a few years before Giotto was born. Giotto first helped his master, Cimabue, with certain paintings there.

Saint Francis Driving the Devils out of Arezzo,
by Giotto di Bondone. Church of Saint Francis,
Assisi, Italy. © Art Resource, NY/Scala.

Saint Francis of Assisi Renouncing his Possessions,
by Giotto di Bondone. Church of Saint Francis,
Assisi, Italy ©Art Resource, NY/Scala.

Several years later, Giotto returned with his own assistants to do more paintings. These paintings are called frescoes. Frescoes are watercolors brushed onto wet plaster. After drying, these paintings last a very long time. Even though many of Giotto's works are cracked and patchy looking today, they're in pretty good shape for being more than 700 years old!

The Dream of Joachim, by Giotto di Bondone. c. 1305-06. Scrovegni Chapel, Padua, Italy.
© Art Resource, NY/Scala.

After doing the St. Francis frescoes, Giotto's next big job was painting forty-one beautiful frescoes in Padua, Italy. He then traveled all over Italy, painting wonderful artwork along the way.

Years later, when Giotto returned to Florence, he decorated the chapel of Santa Croce. Many people think these paintings are his greatest masterpieces.

As he worked on each group of paintings, Giotto tried as hard as he could to create a feeling of real space and make his people seem more and more alive. Everyone in Florence loved the Santa Croce paintings.

Detail of *The Death of Saint Francis*, by Giotto di Bondone. Bardi Chapel, Santa Croce, Florence, Italy. © Art Resource, NY/Scala.

The people of Florence were proud to
have Giotto back home painting. During
this time, the great Italian cities competed
for all kinds of things.

There were battles for power and riches. Everyone wanted their city to be the most beautiful, too. The best artists were considered heroes—just like brave knights or sports stars.

Giotto di Bondone was a pretty brave artist. He broke away from the rules set up by the church leaders when no one else dared to. He modeled his figures after ordinary people he saw in the streets. Giotto made

Saint Francis Preaching to the Birds, by Giotto di Bondone. Church of Saint Francis, Assisi, Italy. © Art Resource, NY/Scala.

Detail of *Nativity,* by Giotto di Bondone. c. 1305-06. Scrovegni Chapel, Padua, Italy. © Archivi Alinari, Firenze. Photograph © Art Resource, NY.

Jesus and his mother Mary look familiar, like someone's neighbor or relative. People found it much easier to learn about religious stories when figures in paintings were more natural looking.

Campanile (Bell Tower) of the Duomo of Florence, by Giotto di Bondone. Exterior view. Florence, Italy. © Art Resource, NY/Scala.

Giotto was not only one of the greatest painters ever, but was also a talented architect. He designed the famous bell tower in Florence, Italy, known to this day as Giotto's Tower.

Giotto died in 1337. He may have influenced more great artists than anyone else. Artists from Leonardo da Vinci and Michelangelo to modern artists like Paul Cezanne and Pablo Picasso have been inspired by Giotto di Bondone.

Works of art in this book can be seen at the following places:

Bardi Chapel, Santa Croce, Florence, Italy
Cathedral, Cefalu, Italy
Church of St. Francis, Assisi, Italy
Metropolitan Museum of Art, New York, New York
Monastery Church, Hosios Loukas, Greece
San Apollinare Nuovo, Ravenna, Italy
Scrovegni Chapel, Padua, Italy
Duomo, Florence, Italy